Miraculous Magic Tricks

COMEDY MAGIC

by Thomas Canavan
Illustrations by David Mostyn

WINDMILL
BOOKS

New York

Published in 2014 by Windmill Books, an Imprint of Rosen Publishing
29 East 21st Street, New York, NY 10010

Copyright © 2014 by Arcturus Publishing Ltd.

First Edition

Author: Thomas Canavan
Editors: Patience Coster and Joe Harris
US Editor: Joshua Shadowens
Illustrations: David Mostyn
Design: Emma Randall

Publisher Cataloging Data

Canavan, Thomas.
Comedy magic / by Thomas Canavan.
 p. cm. — (Miraculous magic tricks)
Includes index.
ISBN 978-1-4777-9061-8 (library binding) —
ISBN 978-1-4777-9062-5 (pbk.) —
 ISBN 978-1-4777-9063-2 (6-pack)
1. Magic tricks —Juvenile literature. I. Canavan, Thomas, 1956–. II. Title.
GV 1548.C216 2014
793.8—dc23

Printed in the USA

CPSIA Compliance Information: Batch #BW14WM: For further information contact Windmill Books, New York, New York at 1-866-478-0556
SL003845US

CONTENTS

INTRODUCTION

Within these pages you will discover great magic tricks that are easy to do and impressive to watch.

To be a successful magician, you will need to practice the tricks in private before you perform them in front of an audience. An excellent way to practice is in front of a mirror, since you can watch the magic happen before your own eyes.

When performing, you must speak clearly, slowly, and loudly enough for everyone to hear. But never tell the audience what's going to happen.

Remember to "watch your angles." This means being careful about where your spectators are standing or sitting when you are performing. The best place is directly in front of you.

Never tell the secret of how the trick is done. If someone asks, just say: "It's magic!"

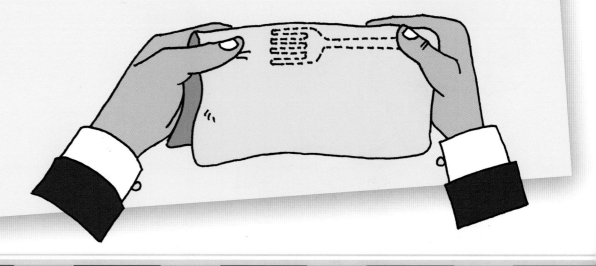

THE MAGICIAN'S PLEDGE

I promise not to reveal the secrets of magic to those who are not magicians.

I promise to practice these magic tricks over and over again before attempting to perform them in front of an audience.

I promise to respect my art, the art of magic.

SHOCKING STRAW

1 The magician sits behind a table and sets a drinking straw in front of him. It should be laid about half an arm's length away.

ILLUSION

The magician uses a "special magnetic force" in his fingertips to move a straw without touching it.

2 The magician says he will use "the magnetic force of static electricity" to push the straw away from him.

3 The magician rubs his index finger through his hair, saying he is building up the electrical charge.

4 He holds this finger over the middle of the straw, without touching it. He moves his finger forward slowly. As he does so, he secretly blows on his side of the straw. The magician takes care not to change the expression on his face as he blows. He stops moving his finger and blowing at the same time.

5 Finally he calls for volunteers from the audience to try the trick. They all fail!

BOUNCING APPLE

ILLUSION

The magician bounces an apple off the floor as if it were a rubber ball.

1 A table and chair are needed for this trick. A low table or even a desk works, as long as the spectators can't see the magician's feet.

2 The trick begins with the magician sitting behind the table with an apple in front of him.

3 He picks up the apple and acts as if he's about to take a bite from it. He stops, sniffs it and says: "Maybe this one isn't ripe. I'd better test it."

4 He holds the apple at shoulder height ...

5 ...then he brings it down quickly, so that it goes out of the spectators' sight behind the table.

6 While doing this, the magician does two more things at the same time: he taps his foot on the ground and flips his wrist so that the apple flicks up in the air.

7 It sounds—and looks—as though the apple has bounced off the floor and back into the air.

8 The magician catches the apple. He says: "Good bounce—it must be ripe!" and takes a bite from it.

UNFOLDABLE TOWEL

ILLUSION

The magician tries to fold an ordinary hand towel but it keeps bulging in unlikely directions.

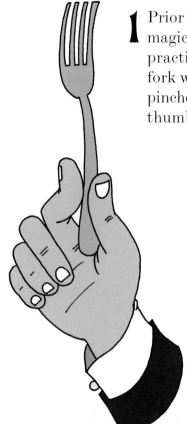

1 Prior to the trick, the magician gets some practice holding a table fork with the handle pinched between his thumb and index finger.

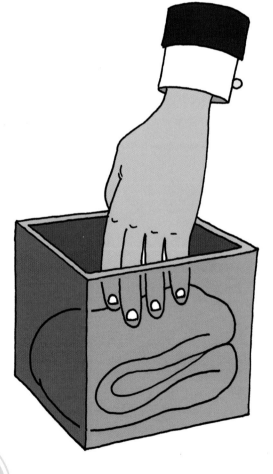

2 To perform the trick, the magician reaches into a box containing "an ordinary hand towel." But a fork is hidden in the towel.

12

3 The magician picks up the towel, continuing to hide the fork by folding the towel over it and holding one end of the fold in his right hand. He holds the other end of the fold in his left hand. (This takes practice!)

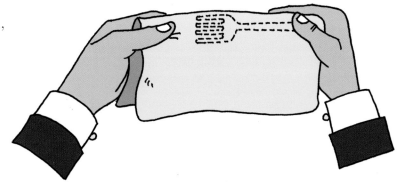

4 The magician shows the towel to the audience, still holding it tight with both hands. The fork can't be seen under the fold. The magician shows the audience the front and back of the towel, like a bullfighter twirling his cape.

5 He tries to fold the towel, twisting his right wrist slightly so that the fork pokes into the fold and makes the towel rise up.

6 The magician looks surprised, and lets the fork go back down again. He continues raising and lowering the towel, staring at it as though he can't believe his eyes.

7 The magician finishes the trick by seeming to scrunch up the towel, but he's really scrunching it around the fork.

8 He puts the scrunched-up towel (with the fork hidden inside) back in the box.

THE STICKY SPOON

ILLUSION

A spoon seems to be stuck magically to the palm of the magician's hand.

1 For this trick, the magician needs to wear a long-sleeved shirt that will cover a wristwatch.

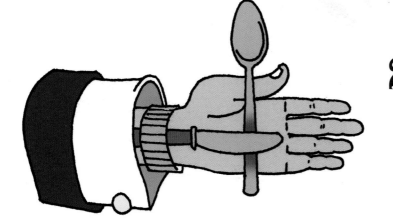

2 Prior to the trick, he slides a butter-knife under his watch-strap so that the blade is snug against the palm of his left hand. Next he slides the handle of a spoon under the blade of the knife. The ends of the spoon should jut out above and below the magician's palm.

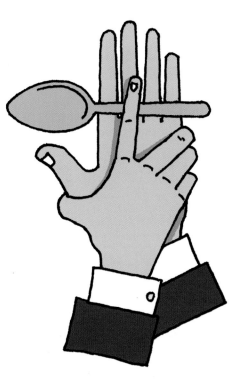

3 To begin the trick, the magician grabs his left wrist with his right hand so that his fingers are pointing in the same direction. He stretches out his right index finger to cover the knife blade.

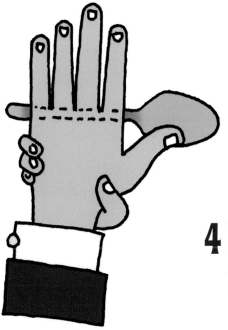

4 The magician holds up his hands so that the spectators see the spoon "stuck" behind his left hand.

5 Still holding his hands together, he turns them to show the other side. The audience can see that his right finger was holding the spoon in place. So he says: "OK—you saw through that one—I'll have to try something else!"

6 Keeping his hands together, the magician turns them back to their original position. Then he removes his right hand and waves it. The spoon is still stuck to his left hand!

BOUNCING HANKIE

ILLUSION

*The magician pulls out
a handkerchief to mop
his brow. He throws
it to the ground, but it
bounces back up again!*

1 Prior to the trick, the magician
finds a very bouncy ball
(about the size of a golf ball).

2 He wraps the ball in a thin
handkerchief and stuffs
it into his pocket.

19

3 On completing the previous trick, the magician says, "Phew—that was tiring! I need to mop my brow." He pulls the handkerchief out of his pocket. Without opening it, he uses it to mop his brow.

4 Then he throws the handkerchief straight down onto the hard floor, as if he's getting rid of it.

5 The handkerchief bounces back up, and the magician catches it and puts it back in his pocket.

6 Keeping a straight face, he says, "Now—where was I?" and moves on to the next trick.

MAGIC TIP!
MAGICIANS CALL QUICK TRICKS "THROWAWAY GAGS." THIS EASY TRICK IS A THROWAWAY GAG THAT ALWAYS GETS A LAUGH!

THE WRONG CARD

ILLUSION

The spectator picks a card, then the deck is placed in a bag. The magician keeps selecting the wrong card and gets so frustrated that he stamps on the bag. When he pulls his foot out, the chosen card is stuck to the bottom of his shoe!

1 Prior to the trick, the magician chooses a card and places it in the deck second from the top. He tapes a duplicate card to the bottom of his shoe, face side up.

2 To perform the trick, the magician places the cards face down and splits the deck in half, placing the halves side by side.

3 He takes the first card from the top half of the deck and places it on the bottom half. He now asks a spectator to pick the next card in the pile (the prepared card). The spectator looks at it, remembers it and shuffles it back into the deck.

4 The magician puts the deck into a large, strong bag. He shakes the bag well.

5 The magician reaches into the bag with his right hand. He pulls out a random card and shows it proudly, before discovering it's the wrong card.

6 He tries again with his left hand, but he still fails to find the spectator's card. Now he's angry! He puts his foot in the bag and stomps on the cards.

7 When he pulls his foot out, the correct card is stuck to the bottom of his shoe!

MAGIC TIP
IF YOU PULL OUT THE RIGHT CARD EARLY ON, STOP AND TAKE A BOW. YOU HAVE JUST PERFORMED MAGIC!

THIMBLE ON THE GO

1 The magician slips a thimble onto the middle finger of his right hand. He makes sure the spectators see him do this.

2 He rests the index and middle fingers of his right hand against the palm of his left hand. Again, he makes sure the spectators see this.

3 The magician says that he will make the thimble jump from one finger to another on the count of three.

ONE...TWO... THREE!

4 He taps his index and middle fingers against his left palm three times, counting "one," "two," "three." Between taps he raises his right hand about one hand's length above his left.

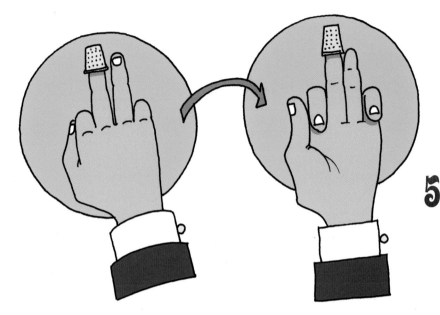

5 On the third tap, as he lowers his right hand, he curls his index finger under and extends his third finger.

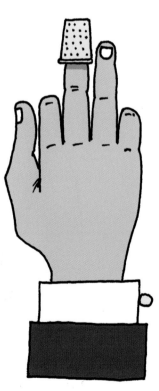

6 This makes it look as though the thimble has jumped fingers.

CRAZY CANDLE

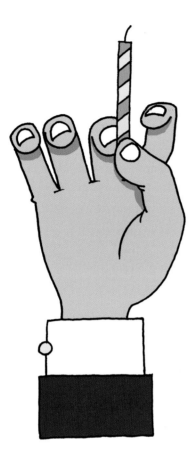

ILLUSION

The magician tells the spectators he can light a candle just by concentrating on it. He holds it tight up against his forehead, opens his hand— and there's a big surprise!

1 The magician holds up a small birthday candle in his right hand. He pinches it slightly with his thumb and middle finger. His palm should be facing away from the spectators.

2 He tells the spectators that he can light the candle just by concentrating on it. The magician looks hard at the candle for a few seconds. Nothing happens. "Hmm . . ." he says. "I need to concentrate a little harder—I'll put the candle closer to my brain." He continues to hold the candle in the same way.

28

3 "Right—now!" he says and, in a motion to move the candle closer to his head, he passes his left hand in front of the candle. As he does this, the magician loosens his grip. The candle falls into his right palm and he closes his hand over it. At the same time he closes his left hand (so it appears that the left hand is now clasped around the candle.)

4 The motion with the left hand finishes at the magician's forehead. He says, "Now I can really concentrate." He looks at the spectators and says: "Help me to concentrate hard on this candle and we can get it to light." As the spectators look up at the magician's left hand, he lowers his right hand and secretly drops the candle.

5 The magician says: "On the count of three, I'll open my hand and the candle will be lit. One ... two ... THREE!" He opens his hand, but there's nothing there! The magician says: "Whoops! Wrong trick!"

PECULIAR PIGGY BANK

ILLUSION
The magician holds up a plastic bottle and seems to "deposit" a coin in it—even though the cap is tightly shut.

1 Prior to the trick, the magician finds a clear plastic bottle with a twist-off cap. Then he finds two identical coins—but these coins must be smaller than the plastic bottle cap.

2 Next he uses clear tape to stick one of the coins to the underside of the bottle cap. He then screws the cap back on, so the bottle is shut tight. He puts the other coin in his pocket.

3 The magician is ready to perform the trick. He holds up the empty bottle and says, "Some people use piggy banks to save their money. I prefer a clear, plastic bottle so I can see what's in there."

4 He then says, "Hmm—this one's empty. I'd better make a deposit." He takes the coin from his pocket and shows it to the audience.

5 "I'm in a hurry so I don't have time to unscrew the cap…" and the magician slaps the coin against the side of the bottle.

6 He quickly shows the bottle to the audience. The first coin has been knocked off the bottom of the cap and is rattling around. The magician waves the bottle towards the audience and pockets the other coin while they are distracted.

FURTHER READING

Barnhart, Norm. *Amazing Magic Tricks.* Mankato, MN: Capstone Press, 2009.

Cassidy, John and Michael Stroud. *Klutz Book of Magic.* Palo Alto, CA: Klutz Press, 2006.

Charney, Steve. *Cool Card Tricks.* Easy Magic Tricks. Mankato, MN: Capstone Press, 2010.

Klingel, Cynthia. *Card Tricks.* Games Around the World. Mankato, MN: Compass Point Books, 2002.

Longe, Bob. *The Little Giant Book of Card Tricks.* New York: Sterling Publishers Inc, 2000.

WEBSITES

For web resources related to the subject of this book, go to: www.windmillbooks.com/weblinks and select this book's title.

GLOSSARY

deposit (dih-PAH-zit) To put something precious somewhere special to keep it safe.

duplicate (DOO-plih-ket) An object that is exactly the same as another object.

index finger (IN-deks FIN-gur) The finger next to the thumb.

static electricity (STA-tik ih-lek-TRIH-suh-tee) A force that can pull objects together, push them apart, or create sparks.

thimble (THIM-buhl) A metal finger protector.

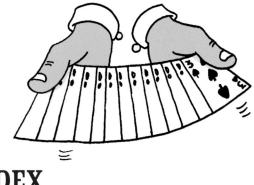

INDEX